PULLET SURPRISES

Amsel Greene

PULLET

SURPRISES

"In 1952," wrote a high school lad,
"Eugene O'Neill won a Pullet Surprise"

by AMSEL GREENE

Illustrations by the author

SULTANA PRESS   FULLERTON, CALIFORNIA   1969

Copyright © 1969, by Amsel Greene

This book or parts thereof may not be reproduced
in any form without written permission of the author
or her agent, except in the case of brief quotations
embodied in critical articles and reviews.

For information, write
PULLET SURPRISES
747-A AVENIDA MAJORCA
LAGUNA HILLS, CALIFORNIA 92653

Printed in the United States of America

To my sister, Eula Greene Miller, who shared with me the work and the fun of choosing the Pullet Surprises to appear in this book, and whose encouragement in any enterprise has been my chief blessing always.

Acknowledgment

I am deeply indebted to my former high school students who unknowingly made this book possible—from the Happy-Go-Lucky Minority, who couldn't be bothered with differentiation between words, to the Purposeful Majority, who met the challenge of unknown words with a logic and an ingenuity that made misinterpretations truly admirable. The Pullet Surprises of this book are offered not in ridicule, but in a desire to share their delight with readers who will relish them, *including* those former students from whose papers they were gleaned.

A.G.

To the Reader

If you are a proponent of speed reading, pass this book by. If you enjoy pausing as you read, to smile, reflect, or comment, read on.

The author suggests that you read the Introduction through, at one brief sitting, to sample the types of classroom Pullet Surprises you will meet in the four sections of the book. Reserve the individual chapters for casual, pick-up reading thereafter, preferably in sequence. Try the Guessing Games at the ends of chapters not more than one or two at a time, for fun or diversion. The Appendix offers additional Guessing Games of each type.

Throughout the book, sentences by which students have tried to clarify or justify their definitions are enclosed in quotation marks, the possible comments or observations of readers, in parentheses.

Most of the Pullet Surprises herein were garnered from the yearly preliminary tests taken by students entering the author's classes in vocabulary building. Some, however, were the later results of a little learning mistakenly applied. The author's respect and affection for her students would not permit her to dismiss surprising definitions as senseless. Instead, she tried to trace the reasoning which may have led to unorthodox conclusions. In Chapter 5 she points the way, and invites you to participate in such amusing probing.

Contents

Introduction

What *is* a Pullet Surprise?

derelict	a queer way of speaking	"We found it hard to understand his Scottish derelict."
amnesia	a medicine	"The doctor said to take some milk of amnesia."
cursory	inclined to swear	"Fred's mother used to wash out his mouth with soap, to curb his cursory tendencies."
diffident	return on an investment	"He expects to retire and live on his diffident."
cynic	picturesque	"The Rocky Mountain road was the most cynic of our entire trip."

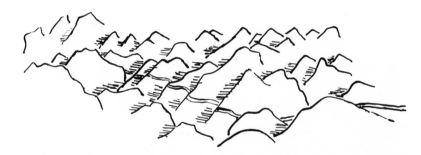

These are Pullet Surprises. The name is the unwitting contribution of a high school student whose teacher shared with me a paper in which he had written, "In 1957 Eugene O'Neill won a Pullet Surprise."

A Pullet Surprise! Here was the term for which I had been groping. As the teacher of a high school course in vocabulary building, I had jotted down hundreds of classroom misinterpretations, for which I had found no name. The terms *boners, bloopers, and boo-boos* imply stupidity or inadvertence, whereas student errors are often marvels of ingenuity and logic. *Howlers* would exclude those refreshing interpretations that evoke a chuckle, not a shout. I had rejected all customary designations as unsuitable.

But *Pullet Surprise* sparked a Eureka response. Its rightness had the impact of revelation. Every misinterpretation is by nature a surprise; the word *pullet* is from the Latin *pullus*, meaning a young animal; the most engaging of young animals are those in our high schools. *Of course* their errors are *Pullet Surprises!*

Experience convinces me that in general the Pullet Surprises of high school students spring from one or the other of two characteristic traits of youth: untroubled confidence in what they *think* they know, *or* the courage to face and conquer what they realize they do *not* know. For example, overconfidence engendered:

psychic

psychic	a person's build	"The athlete was extremely proud of his psychic."
dissent	line of ancestry	"The knight was of noble dissent."

The will to meet the challenge of the unknown is responsible for

homogeneous	handy man around the house
adage	advanced age
stalemate	husband or wife no longer interesting.

adage

A Pullet Surprise may be an interpretation widely shared; it may be a never-to-be-duplicated product of a unique brain wave. For example, Pathé is obviously the source of the recurrent assumption that *pathology* means the study of news events, but not more than one student in a decade would figure out that *diurnal* must mean two-jugged.

As a collection of misinterpretations grows, distinctions emerge that tend to subdivide both the general and the unique. It becomes evident that Pullet Surprises are the product of distinctive patterns of thinking by which students— and adults—may be grouped.

In one group are the Happily Unaware, who mistake one word for another of somewhat similar sound or appearance:

monetary	a place where monks live
antithesis	something administered before surgery
paradox	a lovely place to go when you die

antithesis One who thus fails to distinguish between similarity and identity in words is enviably self-assured. His reading is untroubled. To him the mention of Robert Louis Stevenson as a *valetudinarian* is clear proof of the author's excellent scholarship; to him the books in an *eclectic* library are unquestionably in the field of the physical sciences; to him *posterity* means wealth, and he appreciates accordingly the concern of the makers of the Constitution "for ourselves and our posterity."

A subdivision of the Unaware is made up of the many who are insensitive in listening and slipshod in speech:

"The church is holding a series of revile meetings."
"When he retires he will get a penchant."

In contrast to the Happily Unaware are the Uneasily Aware. These are alert to non-identity in words, but hold resemblances suspect. They feel obliged to justify any similarity:

idiom	a sanitarium for the ill in mind
alienist	a naturalized citizen
deciduous	able to make up one's mind quickly

Such definitions, born of the labored thought of the Uneasily Aware, are the most admirable of all Pullet Surprises. Confronted with a word totally unknown, the student marshals all his resources in an effort to extract meaning. His reasoning leads to deductions in no way resembling the hasty certainties of the Happily Unaware. For example, the youth who defined *lassitude* as distance crosswise was obviously thinking of lassitude and longitude, but the one who defined *lassitude* as girlishness had thought a problem through.

In a third and smaller group are the Nonchalant. These have neither the assurance of the first group nor the concern of the second. Their interpretations follow no discernible pattern, and defy analysis:

eulogy	study of the veins and muscles
prognosticate	force one into something
atheist	one of the white race

A fourth and extensive group is composed of the Trusting. These rely upon their ability to divine meanings from usage and context. Since an erroneous assumption drawn from one context is frequently confirmed by subsequent usages, correction may be long delayed. Meantime, the Trusting are likely to defend vigorously a meaning repeatedly taken for granted:

prodigal	wandering
anonymous	annoying
orthodox	characteristic of the middle-aged

A section of this book will be given to the Pullet Surprises of each of the four groups described. All are unaltered interpretations met in the author's classes. Naive or ingenious, baffling or understandable, all are genuine Pullet Surprises.

Do you enjoy puzzles and games? At the ends of most chapters in this book, Pullet Surprise Guessing Games invite you to try your skill, alone or in competition, at matching words with classroom definitions. Avid puzzle fans will find additional games in the Appendix.

The composite Guessing Game below sets the pattern. Column A lists words students were asked to define. These are designated by numbers. Column B lists student definitions, *not* in the order of the words in Column A. Definitions are designated by letters. You are to match the lettered definitions with the numbered words, *and* guess the word responsible for the student's misinterpretation.

To play the game, follow these steps:

1. For each Word in Column A, find the most likely teen-ager Definition in Column B.

2. In the parentheses after the Word in Column A, write the letter designating the Definition you have chosen.

3. In the parentheses after your chosen Definition, write the word you judge responsible for the student's confusion.

EXAMPLE: In the Guessing Game below, you are given a three-word start.

PULLET SURPRISE GUESSING GAME 1.

COLUMN A		COLUMN B	
WORD		STUDENT DEFINITION	
1. bizarre	(g)	a. sorry for some one	( )
2. monger	(d)	b. small insect on plants	( )
3. cliché	(i)	c. a rule in math	( )
4. solon	( )	d. a dog, not pedigreed	(mongrel)
5. synthetic	( )	e. an editor	( )
6. fiasco	( )	f. a beauty parlor	( )
7. relevant	( )	g. a church sale	(bazaar)
8. publican	( )	h. a wall painting	( )
9. idiom	( )	i. a group of snobs	(clique)
10. avid	( )	j. aunt, uncle, cousin, etc.	( )

When you have filled all blanks, check your answers with those of the footnote. Footnote answers give Word number, matching letter, and word evidently responsible for the misinterpretation.

ANSWERS:

ANSWERS TO GUESSING GAME 1

1. g (bazaar)	6. h (fresco)
2. d (mongrel)	7. j (relative)
3. i (clique)	8. e (publisher)
4. f (salon)	9. c (axiom)
5. a (sympathetic)	10. b (aphid)

THE

HAPPILY

UNAWARE

"Nothing to it!"

1   Mistaken Identity

THE HAPPILY UNAWARE constantly provide a fresh supply of Pullet Surprises by simply mistaking one word for another. A definition or usage of the one usually reveals the identity of the other:

prognosticate	to put off
hypothesis	long side of a right triangle
paragon	Bible story with a moral

Teen-agers frequently add to a definition what they consider a clarifying explanation or illustration:

WORD	TEEN-AGER DEFINITION	CLARIFICATION (?)
monetary	for the moment	"Monetarily disturbed, he quickly regained his composure."
divulge	flood	"Many were floundering in the great divulge."
matriculate	particular	"Aunt Phoebe is a matriculate housekeeper."
paradox	imitation	"His paradox on the national anthem aroused a protest."
solon	place where drinks are sold	"The drunkard could usually be found in the vicinity of a solon."
pathos	coins	"He paid many pathos for the rare painting."
avid	full of life	"I like avid colors."
dissimulation	scattering	"Wide dissimulation of their ideas is the Communist plan."
levity	taxes	"April 15 is the day of levity in the United States."

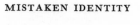

WORD	TEEN-AGER DEFINITION	CLARIFICATION (?)
cliché	grip; hold	"She didn't like to dance with him because of his tight cliché."
compunction	force	"The attorney claimed that the will had been signed under compunction."
simulate	vigorize	"Coffee simulates."
vindictive	one of the moods in grammar	"There are four—subjunctive, imperative, vindictive, and one I can't remember."
suppliant	flexible	"Exercise keeps the body suppliant."
virulent	strong and healthy	"The coach picked only the most virulent players for the first team."

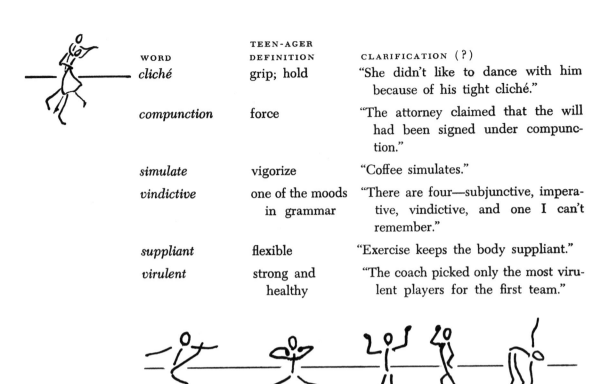

The word with which another is confused may not be instantly apparent:

innuendo	fading away	"She played the final movement innuendo."
emaciate	set free	"Have you read the Emaciation Proclamation?"
atheist	a jewel	"He asked whether she'd rather have a ruby or an atheist, and she said an atheist."
peccadillo	a bull fighter	"The vast crowd watched breathless as the famous peccadillo teased and angered the bull."

Mistakes in identity may have to be inferred from student usage alone. Arresting usages often inspire listener comment:

TEEN-AGER USAGE	LISTENER COMMENT
"She paid her intuition fee."	(One has to pay for everything these days.)
'The lieutenant was well trained in marital maneuvers."	(The armed services are constantly expanding their activities.)
"Annually the club names its man of Extinction."	(A coveted honor?)
"By the time the police found him, metamorphosis had set in."	(Must the police cope with *that?*)
"Above all, she wanted Elvis Presley's epitaph."	(She's not alone.)
"She contributed her corpulence to a nearby candy shop."	(An admirable solution!)
"The Constitution provides that no alienist shall ever become president of the United States."	(What contingency did the framers anticipate?)
"This camera is equipped with an aseptic lens."	(Should be required in all movie and TV photography.)

Definitions alone may evoke like comment:

polygamy   a dread disease   (Dr. Salk! Calling Dr. Salk!)

chicanery   something they mix with coffee to make it go farther.   (Often!)

posterity   success   (Agreed.)

The Pullet Surprises in the Guessing Games that follow are of the Mistaken Identity type. Try your skill at recognition. Game procedures are uniform throughout the book. (see page 18) The words of Column A are to be matched with classroom definitions in Column B. Answers will be found on page 24. Games 4 and 5 of the *Mistaken Identity* type, and answers, will be found in the Appendix.

PULLET SURPRISE GUESSING GAME 2

	COLUMN A				COLUMN B
	WORD				STUDENT DEFINITION
1.	posterity	(	)	a.	baby clothes
2.	illegible	(	)	b.	get money by blackmail
3.	magnate	(	)	c.	a newspaper
4.	chronic	(	)	d.	a platform
5.	laity	(	)	e.	part of the eye
6.	tome	(	)	f.	not qualified
7.	travail	(	)	g.	back portion
8.	retinue	(	)	h.	burial place
9.	nostrum	(	)	i.	a worm
10.	exhort	(	)	j.	go places

chronic!

travail

PULLET SURPRISE GUESSING GAME 3

	COLUMN A				COLUMN B
	WORD				STUDENT DEFINITION
1.	bolster	(	)	a.	beautiful building in Greece
2.	corroborate	(	)	b.	stretch out
3.	necropolis	(	)	c.	a tank
4.	bequest	(	)	d.	think over
5.	debilitate	(	)	e.	a wine
6.	extenuate	(	)	f.	something with a pull
7.	cognate	(	)	g.	work together
8.	dilemma	(	)	h.	pocket in belt for gun
9.	skeptic	(	)	i.	ask
10.	magnate	(	)	j.	what you get when you graduate

dilemma

ANSWERS TO GUESSING GAMES:

GAME 3

1. h (holster)
2. g (collaborate)
3. a (Acropolis)
4. i (request)
5. d (deliberate)
6. b (extend)
7. e (cognac)
8. j (diploma)
9. c (septic)
10. f (magnet)

GAME 2

1. g (posterior)
2. f (ineligible)
3. i (maggot)
4. c (chronicle)
5. a (layette)
6. h (tomb)
7. j (travel)
8. e (retina)
9. d (rostrum)
10. b (extort)

2 *Blurrish*

CASUAL LISTENING and careless pronunciation are responsible for a special group of Mistaken Identity interpretations, a group both amusing and disquieting. All about us we hear a blurred language that bears a disturbing resemblance to English. The words are approximations of those we know; the speech, obviously *related* to English, we shall call Blurrish:

"Every car is equipped with a corroborator."

"His abominable pains were caused by ulcers."

Where Blurrish is spoken, Pullet Surprises abound. Some of them tax the credulity of the uninitiated, but we who encounter them daily become inured to such definitions as

vituperation   "a violet announcement"

We resist the temptation to pursue the potentialities of a violet announcement, and instead try to account for the phrase. Experience has sharpened perception, and we divine that an oral definition

vituperation   a violent denouncement

has been heard—and accepted without question—as a violet announcement.

With practice we grow adept at recognition when we hear that a new family is moving in next store, or that the Glee Club is currently rehearsing the song about the Vulgar Boatman. We appreciate an offer of information about partial post rates, and learn without surprise that if we when to the libery we could find the year the electric light pulp was invented, and the name of the best-seller recently decaded to the Precedent. We sympathize with older sisters who consider younger brothers nuances, and are interested but not alarmed when warned that people living in frame houses should watch for hermits that sometimes bore through walls and weaken the structure. Once conditioned, we take in stride the revelation that Crusoe, in addition to his other proficiencies, was a noted tenor, or the assertion that the most famous ascetic of our generation was Mott McGondy, whom Nero succeeded as leader of India's millions. So infectious is Blurrish that we begin to suspect that by the time we intrepid a few such paragraphs we shall need a sediment, and that, rather we do or not, it is comforting to be assured that we can get one at the coroner drug.

Examples of Blurrish frequently crop up in sentences illustrating an orthodox definition:

WORD	TEEN-AGER DEFINITION	CLARIFICATION (?)
impetuous	acting on impulse	"Most idle essents are impetuous at times."

A thought-provoking observation! Evidently the plaint that high school students don't want to study is unfair. How can they when they are at the idle essent stage? And no wonder they don't know what to make of that occasional anomaly, an energetic essent!

In the home, on the air, everywhere, lazy speech is creating a verbal smog threatening to envelop our language. Not many speakers are *incapable* of accuracy in enunciation; most of the guilty are simply content with approximation. A few even deliberately blur speech in the unworthy fear that precision may be deemed affectation. And the smog is gaining. Through it the English version of a Blurrish statement can usually be dimly discerned:

"The whole world was shaken by the attack on Peril Harbor."

"Our new school has a four stair heating system."

"His prior surface made him certain of the promotion."

"Antibiotics are supposed to contract diseases."

"Exhilaration makes a high-powered car dangerous in the hands of any one just learning to drive."

"John Hancock's sinecure is the plainest on the Declaration of Independence."

When a definition accompanies a Blurrish statement, it helps to penetrate the haze:

eulogize	make use of	"Rug makers eulogize every scrap of material."
ominous	something to ride in	"In stories of London, people are always boarding an ominous."
gregarious	a calendar	"Before our present calendar was adopted, the Gregarious calendar was used."

WORD	TEEN-AGER DEFINITION	CLARIFICATION (?)
malady	a tune	"Some folks prefer any of the old-time maladies to Rock-and-Roll."
surfeit	ocean waves	"Visitors to the Islands marvel at the surfeit riders."
ephemeral	womanish	"To me he seems rather ephemeral."
amiable	able to be taken away	"Jefferson said that all men are born with inamiable rights."
invective	not getting results	"All medicines have proved invective against this disease."
pensive	not yet granted	"The label says, 'Patent Pensive'."
ogre	to eye	"He stood there and ogred the girls going by."
strident	a three-pronged wand	"Neptune is always pictured with his strident."

Blurrish tends to get out of bounds:

equivocate	leave a place in a hurry	"The soldiers equivocated the camp within an hour."
cursory	paper money	"He had some silver in his pocket, but most of his money was cursory."
chronic	a winder	"It took a chronic to start the first Model T's."

Nothing is impossible:

anomaly	very small	"We paid anomaly fee."
colloquial	church	"His friends went to the public school, but he was sent to a colloquial school."
maudlin	a kind of cotton cloth	"The store had a special on fine, maudlin sheets."
Alamo	ice cream on top	"People are always saying, 'Remember the Alamo'."

Students who speak Blurrish are quickly identified when asked to use words in sentences:

WORD	TEEN-AGER USAGE
centaur	"Every state is permitted to send two centaurs to Congress."
tycoon	"The tycoon raged in the islands for two days and nights."
surreptitious	"She was surreptitious about black cats."
innovation	"The speaker received quite innovation."
levity	" 'One nation under God, indivisible, with levity and justice for all.' "
derision	"Ted is good in multiplication and derision."
austerity	"The Constitution ensures certain rights to 'ourselves and our austerity'."

Even in its advanced stages Blurrish is unlikely to startle the experienced listener:

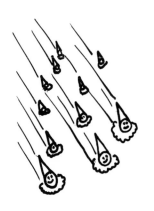

Camelot	"In the Sarah Desert they travel by Camelot."
opulent	"The opulents on his shoulders showed his military rank."
purloin	"American prisoners dreamed of ice cream and purloin steaks."
perfidy	"The princess mounted her spirited perfidy and rode away."
chivalry	"He drives a red Chivalry."
comic	"Space flying may be affected by comic rays."

Almost any example of Blurrish may trigger question or comment:

TEEN-AGER USAGE	LISTENER COMMENT
"Geometry was invented by Eucalyptus."	(All branches?)
"The caustics of the theater were excellent."	(Actors, beware!)
"Mr. Graham is our local weather procrastinator."	(Every community needs one.)
"Way out in the woods we came upon a dissolute old cabin."	(Plainly tipsy?)
"Her accessories were in quiet good taste. She usually wore a single pedant on a gold chain."	(More than one *would* have been conspicuous.)
"His father's inspiration and affluence guided his whole life."	(Affluence does help.)
"It was only a surface scratch but already information had set in."	(Teachers, take heart.)
"The audience was restlessly awaiting the rile of the speaker."	(Patience. It may not take long.)
"It all started with the Adam Balm."	(Eve?)
"Moses went up on Mt. Cyanide to get the Decalogue."	(He took a risk.)
"You learn about that in alimentary school."	(Calories, proteins, and such?)
"One of the Ten Commandments says, 'Thou shalt not covert'."	(We'd be interested in hearing the other nine.)
"Charivari is dead."	(No comment.)
"She puts on airs, but she's always making social plunders."	(She'll get along!)
"The vassal held three barrels of beer."	(Must be a record.)
"The banker's money was well infested."	(H-m-m-m-m.)
"The Hydrogen Bomb is often called the Itch Bomb. I don't know why."	(Nor I.)

Definitions alone may evoke similar response:

WORD	TEEN-AGER DEFINITION	LISTENER COMMENT
antipathy	looking forward to	(Like children antipathating a circus?)
apathy	uncomplimentary term	(As when a witness uses an objectionable apathy in describing the accused?)
depravity	poverty	(Depraved of necessities?)
dissipation	requirement for doctor's degree	(How long has it been *required?*)
chameleon	a country in the King Arthur stories	(Where he had his Round Table. Remember?)
scrupulous	surgical	(Needle! Scrupul! Sponge! Clamp!)

Are you ready for Guessing Games in Blurrish? Try those on the following pages before looking at the answers on pages 31 and 32. Games 9 to 13 of the Blurrish type will be found in the Appendix.

PULLET SURPRISE GUESSING GAME — 6

COLUMN A			COLUMN B		
WORD			**STUDENT DEFINITION**		
1. cable	(	)	a. a field of poppies	(	)
2. invective	(	)	b. intention	(	)
3. deify	(	)	c. a kind of mixed pickle	(	)
4. innate	(	)	d. a debate	(	)
5. deference	(	)	e. unsigned	(	)
6. porpoise	(	)	f. take a stand against	(	)
7. philander	(	)	g. answer when you subtract	(	)
8. anomalous	(	)	h. efficient	(	)
9. peccadillo	(	)	i. contagious	(	)
10. augment	(	)	j. person in an institution	(	)

deference

PULLET SURPRISE GUESSING GAME — 7

COLUMN A			COLUMN B		
WORD			**STUDENT DEFINITION**		
1. incipient	(	)	a. before the second and third	(	)
2. elegy	(	)	b. feel like yelling whoopee	(	)
3. dudgeon	(	)	c. entering a country by force	(	)
4. adjunct	(	)	d. cause of rashes, etc.	(	)
5. exalt	(	)	e. a dark prison	(	)
6. envision	(	)	f. a shot a nurse gives you	(	)
7. trite	(	)	g. Hitler	(	)
8. hippodrome	(	)	h. word that describes	(	)
9. foist	(	)	i. uninteresting	(	)
10. furor	(	)	j. something that goes on and on in one family for generations	(	)

hippodrome

exalt

ANSWERS TO GUESSING GAMES:

GAME 6

1. h (capable)
2. i (infective)
3. f (defy)
4. j (inmate)
5. g (difference)
6. b (purpose)
7. a (Flanders)
8. e (anonymous)
9. c (piccalilli)
10. d (argument)

GAME 7

1. i (insipid)
2. d (allergy)
3. e (dungeon)
4. h (adjective)
5. b (exult)
6. c (invasion)
7. j (trait)
8. f (hypodermic)
9. a (first)
10. g (Fuehrer)

COLUMN A			COLUMN B		
WORD			STUDENT DEFINITION		
1. veracity	(	)	a. a hobo, drifter	(	)
2. salient	(	)	b. a showy flower	(	)
3. facile	(	)	c. a thin cooky	(	)
4. chameleon	(	)	d. attacker	(	)
5. matriculate	(	)	e. one or the other	(	)
6. tenure	(	)	f. fierceness	(	)
7. trenchant	(	)	g. a decade	(	)
8. waiver	(	)	h. something old dug up	(	)
9. parricide	(	)	i. speak each syllable clearly	(	)
10. ethereal	(	)	j. plant or animal living off another	(	)

salient

ANSWERS TO GUESSING GAMES:

GAME 8

1. f (ferocity)
2. d (assailant)
3. h (fossil)
4. b (camellia)
5. i (articulate)
6. g (ten year)
7. a (transient)
8. c (wafer)
9. j (parasite)
10. e (either)

3   The Power of Suggestion

THE HAPPILY UNAWARE, whose interpretations are unclouded by doubt, are responsible for still another group of Pullet Surprises. Something in the sound or appearance of one word has suggested another. The confusion may be the result of snap judgment or of too hasty an appraisal of apparent clues. Typical of snap judgments are:

niggardly	black
longevity	being very tall

Misleading clues suggested:

gubernatorial	to do with peanuts
sardonic	packed together tightly
felicitous	being catty

When a single word suggests a variety of misinterpretations, one can only speculate about the underlying associations:

WORD	TEEN-AGER DEFINITION	READER SPECULATION
parsimonious	preachy	(From *parson?*)
	sour	(From "*parsimmon?*)
	to do with grammar	(From *parsing?*)
	spicy; sharp	(From *parsley?*)
vicarious	wicked	(From *vice?*)
	second in rank	(From vice-president?)

Associations may be suggested by Blurrish clues:

panacea	a container	(A frying panacea?)
entomology	study of mummies	(Long buried?)

WORD	TEEN-AGER DEFINITION	READER SPECULATION
pantomime	a ghost	(A Hallowe'en phantomime?)
dendrology	study of lawn control	(For dendrolions?)
cynic	censor	(Like cynicated newspaper columns?)

Clairvoyant readers will devine the words that suggested the definitions below. Those less perceptive, or less patient, may refer to the footnote:

WORD	TEEN-AGER DEFINITION
prodigal	brilliant
fortuitous	well protected
tyro	a cruel ruler
monger	one who hounds others
vicissitude	glueyness
effusive	able to be merged
amnesty	bird house
exodus	tenth chapter

Students often obligingly "clarify" definitions:

WORD	TEEN-AGER DEFINITION	CLARIFICATION (?)
lugubrious	sticky	"When the baby got into the molasses, she was one lugubrious mess."
spurious	wearing spurs	"The coyboy strode spuriously through the admiring crowd."
tonsorial	of the throat	"Tonsorial operations are often performed with only a local anesthetic."
lurid	come-hither	"She had a lurid smile."
risibility	likelihood of coming up	"Before a voyage one should test the risibility of various foods."
flagrancy	perfumery	"The exclusive store carried only French perfumes in their flagrancy department."
sinister	a criminal	"The sinister finally repented."
divulge	fill to bulging	"After the banquet every one felt divulged."
genealogy	study of how to be pleasing	"Dale Carnegie wrote a book about it."

---

prodigy	tyrant	viscous	nest
fort	mongrel	fuse	X

WORD	TEEN-AGER DEFINITION	CLARIFICATION (?)
lugubrious	cumbersome	"The redcap had trouble with her lugubrious luggage."
archaic	having arches	"We were studying the archaic buildings of Europe."
prognostication	protuberance	"Jimmy Durante's prognostication is a great asset."

lugubrious

Meanings not stated can usually be inferred from the mere usages of words:

"The carpenter tested the levity of the table."
"A vacuum cleaner is a succulent device."
"Children love to feed peanuts to the big taciturns when the circus comes to town."

taciturn

Definitions alone, usages alone, or definitions with explanatory usages may evoke adult comment or question:

Definitions alone:

		READER COMMENT
orthodox	a huge animal	(Plural, orthodoxen?)
enigma	growth or tumor	(Benigmant?)
missive	something sent into outer space	(So far, no answer.)

Usages alone:

TEEN-AGER USAGE	READER COMMENT
"The moat around the castle was full of polyglots."	(The Tower of Babel?)
"My brother likes any kind of camisole dish."	(Men!)

Definitions and usages:

		CLARIFICATION (?) AND READER COMMENT
dilatory	energetic	"The most dilatory employees get the raise." (It happens all the time.)
diabolic	having diabetes	"My aunt's diabolic condition worries the family." (It should.)

The Happily Unaware are especially susceptible to the power of suggestion. Its influence is apparent in the Guessing Games which follow. Success in these Games depends upon recognition of associated ideas. Words which *may* account for the definitions appear as "Answers" at the bottom of this page. Additional games, 16 to 21, of this type will be found in the Appendix.

PULLET SURPRISE GUESSING GAME — 14

COLUMN A		COLUMN B	
WORD		STUDENT DEFINITION	
1. paroxysm	( )	a. sound of the sonic bomb	( )
2. pundit	( )	b. a dumb expression	( )
3. avaricious	( )	c. containing beeswax	( )
4. idiom	( )	d. furnishing power for loco-motives	( )
5. versatile	( )	e. satisfied; happy	( )
6. resonant	( )	f. wisecracker	( )
7. ingenuous	( )	g. bleaching hair	( )
8. boomerang	( )	h. knightly behavior	( )
9. contentious	( )	i. flying planes	( )
10. chauvinism	( )	j. poetic	( )

avaricious

chauvinism

PULLET SURPRISE GUESSING GAME — 15

COLUMN A		COLUMN B	
WORD		STUDENT DEFINITION	
1. impious	( )	a. easily smashed	( )
2. salubrious	( )	b. smartness in dress	( )
3. fiasco	( )	c. monkey-like	( )
4. arbitrary	( )	d. to do with past events	( )
5. combustible	( )	e. devilish	( )
6. sedentary	( )	f. with trees and gardens	( )
7. chicanery	( )	g. feast; festival	( )
8. pariah	( )	h. prim and proper	( )
9. apiary	( )	i. slippery	( )
10. histrionic	( )	j. Bible term for king	( )

impious

apiary

ANSWERS TO GUESSING GAMES:

GAME 14

1. g (peroxide)
2. f (pun)
3. i (aviator)
4. b (idiot)
5. j (verse)
6. c (resin)
7. d (engine)
8. a (boom)
9. e (contented)
10. h (chivalry)

GAME 15

1. e (imp)
2. i (lubricate)
3. g (fiesta)
4. f (arbor)
5. a (bust)
6. h (sedate)
7. b (chic)
8. j (pharaoh)
9. c (ape)
10. d (history)

THE

UNEASILY

AWARE

"Oh, dear!"

4   Noble Effort

SECTION I has presented the Pullet Surprises of the Happily Unaware, who identify one word with another at sight. In Section II we shall sample not snap judgments, but the considered conclusions of students who instantly recognize *non*identity, but who assume that a resemblance between two words must have significance. These students, the Uneasily Aware, do not mistake the unknown word *valetudinarian* for the known word *valedictorian*, but they feel obliged to rationalize the similarity. Deductions vary widely, but all give evidence of noble efforts to ferret out plausible meanings:

> *valetudinarian*
> > one who trains valedictorians
> > **a test to determine the valedictorian**
> > a very high I Q organization admitting only ex-valedictorians

Comparison quickly reveals the difference between a Mistaken Identity and a Noble Effort interpretation:

WORD	MISTAKEN IDENTITY	NOBLE EFFORT
risibility	how far as aviator can see	ability to rise in the world
sinister	an old maid	one who breaks sacred laws
bibliography	story of some one's life	holy geography
acumen	heap up; collect	No such word. Probably a misprint for *vacumen*, a place with no air
tenet	a renter	a group of singers, like a sextet, only ten of them

Sharp lines cannot be drawn between Pullet Surprise categories. One type merges imperceptibly into another. Who can say whether the definition below should be attributed to Suggestion, in instant response to the first two syllables of the word, or to Noble Effort, which may have searched for and utilized a clue:

WORD	TEEN-AGER DEFINITION	CLARIFICATION (?)
amenable	worthy of approval	"The congregation found the minister's words amenable."

Reader comment is almost reflex:

		READER COMMENT
antipodes	before time of podes	(Say in 364 B.P.?)
adamant	pertaining to original sin	(Does Webster, in fairness list *eve*-ant?)
convalescence	stage just after adolescence	(Parents, hold that thought!)

A single word can yield any number of admirably logical Noble Effort interpretations:

dogmatic	powered by dogs
	a dog machine
	allergic to dogs
alienist	one who advocates foreign aid
	one in charge of immigrants
	a divorce attorney

A student may provide an illustration to clinch his definition.

		CLARIFICATION (?)
impassive	not able to be promoted	"Johnny's parents were told that he was impassive."
	can't be topped	"Babe Ruth's record is still impassive."
	blocking the way	"The avalanche on the road was impassive."

A Noble Effort definition sometimes shows evidence of desperation, but never of defeat:

affable	able to be affed
dermatology	study of derms
hypercritical	past tense of hypocrite

Occasionally, Noble Effort, subjected to tremendous strain, arrives at a meaning that merits special listing as an Incredible:

		READER COMMENT
antitheses	voters opposed to these measures	(Some are probably both antitheses *and* antithoses.)
adamant	God's sister	(Who else?)

What conclusions could be more logical than these:

noncommittal	can't be done
desecrate	release classfied information
phonology	study of the art of disguise
ingenious	not very smart; no genius
plutocrat	a dog aristocrat

misogynist	one skilled in misogyn
odyssey	odd sights and doings
impeccable	non-critical
bumptious	not smooth-riding
plutocrat	sort of between a Republican
	and a Democrat

savoir-faire	cut rate for passengers
perfunctory	functioning perfectly
caustic	showing why
nefarious	not distant
finesse	a female fish

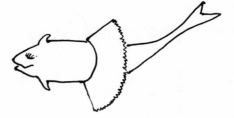

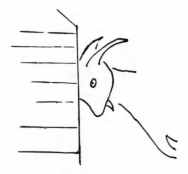

dissent	sent wrong
tenet	a girl tenor
effusive	easily ignited
indolent	not dolent
ramify	hit hard

preponderance	thinking beforehand
exoteric	same as exotic, but even more so
fatuous	overweight
refute	fute over again
expurgate	get out of Purgatory

affluence	opposite of influence
deciduous	determining an issue
jocular	riding race horses
peerage	eyesight
heraldry	journalism

truculent	willing to make a treaty
inveterate	not veterated
cadaverous	carrying golf clubs
recreant	creating repeatedly
diatribe	food plan for whole clan

precursor	reformed blasphemist
polyglot	more than one glot
castanet	method of fishing
neologism	study of lighting
ribaldry	body cage for heart and lungs

homogeneous	devoted to home life
duplicity	being easily duped
strident	taking long steps
ornithology	study of ornies
intestate	remove digestive organs by surgery

parable	able to be equaled
sedentary	very like a sedent
tyro	an Alpine skier
patrimony	same as matrimony, only opposite
doldrums	toy drums

hors d'oeuvre	after hours
impeccable	unable to be dented
tipster	a drunkard
paradox	opposite of orthodox
holocaust	shouting prices at an auction

heliotropic	operating a helicopter
phonology	study of telephone etiquette
orientation	Chinese influence
anathema	a single athema
restive	lazy

hypothesis	one's state after having a hypo
repartee	partying over and over
polyglot	a colony of polygamists
isobar	soda fountain
holocaust	total expense

savant	a preservative
relegate	one re-elected to represent
gullible	to do with sea birds
raillery	travel by train
inherent	deaf

probity	investigation
obnoxious	opposite of noxious
cogitation	what makes some wheels go round
anachronism	belief in the god Anachron
distrait	crooked

intangible	unable to be tangled up
disparaging	non-paraging
bibliophile	a file of Bible characters
dormer	still more dorm
dilatory	place where every one dils

The definitions in the Guessing Games of the following pages are the deductions of serious students, who have recognized the unknown, have grappled with it, and have wrested from it a measure of triumph.

Matching words with Noble Effort definitions may tax your ingenuity. Only after you have exhausted all clues, however, or they have exhausted you, should you check your answers with those at the bottom of the pages. Answers to Guessing Games of the Noble Effort type will give only matching letters and numbers, not the words considered responsible for student deductions. Games 26 to 29 of the Noble Effort type, with answers, will be found in the Appendix.

PULLET SURPRISE GUESSING GAME 22

COLUMN A		COLUMN B
WORD		STUDENT DEFINITION
1. aspirant ( )		a. study of mapping roads
2. bibulous ( )		b. to miss again
3. antithesis ( )		c. two tribes combined
4. stalemate ( )		d. one using aspirin to excess
5. pathology ( )		e. a paper disproving another
6. diatribe ( )		f. slang for Mongolian
7. immutable ( )		g. knowing the Bible well
8. insipid ( )		h. unable to be silenced
9. remiss ( )		i. not fit to drink
10. monger ( )		j. one of the older officers on a ship

monger

PULLET SURPRISE GUESSING GAME 23

COLUMN A		COLUMN B
WORD		STUDENT DEFINITION
1. suppliant ( )		a. non-blasphemous
2. polytechnic ( )		b. under an anesthetic
3. altruism ( )		c. saddle soreness
4. sycophant ( )		d. doctor for infantile paralysis
5. sinecure ( )		e. true in every respect
6. discursive ( )		f. one who meands
7. bronchitis ( )		g. quartermaster
8. meander ( )		h. remedy for sinus trouble
9. plummet ( )		i. person to be sycoanalized
10. ethereal ( )		j. a dwarf variety of prune

bronchitis

ANSWERS TO GUESSING GAMES:

GAME 23		GAME 22	
1. g	6. a	1. d	6. c
2. d	7. c	2. g	7. h
3. e	8. f	3. e	8. i
4. i	9. j	4. j	9. b
5. h	10. b	5. a	10. f

PULLET SURPRISE GUESSING GAME 24

COLUMN A			COLUMN B
WORD			STUDENT DEFINITION
1. prescience	(	)	a. pick some one's pocket
2. ingenuous	(	)	b. clued in
3. discern	(	)	c. week by week
4. clandestine	(	)	d. before the age of science
5. biweekly	(	)	e. make legal again
6. parable	(	)	f. fake; not real
7. disperse	(	)	g. able to be peeled
8. peccadillo	(	)	h. no longer cern
9. relegate	(	)	i. an amateur typist
10. wizened	(	)	j. predestination of a whole tribe

peccadillo

PULLET SURPRISE GUESSING GAME 25

COLUMN A			COLUMN B
WORD			STUDENT DEFINITION
1. redoubtable	(	)	a. nanny goat
2. reprisal	(	)	b. careful beforehand
3. pavilion	(	)	c. repeatedly untrustworthy
4. polemics	(	)	d. strong; unlikely to collapse
5. recreant	(	)	e. lazy; do-nothing
6. precocious	(	)	f. winning award again
7. infallible	(	)	g. branch of track events
8. solarium	(	)	h. one reincarnated
9. noncommittal	(	)	i. a shoe repair shop
10. buttress	(	)	j. way above trillion or quadrillion

1,000,000,000,000,000,000,000,000,000 000
pavilion

ANSWERS TO GUESSING GAMES:

polemics

	GAME 24	GAME 25
1.	d	c
2.	f	f
3.	h	j
4.	j	g
5.	c	h
6.	g	b
7.	a	d
8.	i	i
9.	e	e
10.	b	a

5 Little Learning

WHEN THE MEANING of only a part of a word is known, or mistakenly assumed, a little learning becomes the proverbial hazard, especially when abetted by noble effort. From *monochrome* and *polychrome*, words within his experience, a pupil rightly assumed that *chrom* means color. Subsequently, however, he concluded that the unfamiliar phrase "chromatic scales" must mean "the kind that rainbow trout have."

An incurious reader is likely to dismiss as completely senseless such definitions as

exhume	a ghost
monopoly	E Pluribus Unum
pedantic	crazy dancing
analgesic	explosive

But one experienced in youth's earnest struggles toward meaning is moved to ferret out the "little learning" and the probable reasoning responsible for a baffling conclusion:

WORD	PROBABLE STUDENT REASONING
exhume	"ex — former, as in *ex-president;* hum — person, as in *human being; exhume* — exhuman; a ghost"
monopoly	"mono — one, as in *monotone;* poly — many, as in *polygon; monopoly* — one from many, or E Pluribus Unum"
pedantic	"ped — foot, as in *quadruped;* antic — caper; *pedantic* — foot capering, or crazy dancing"
analgesic	"On radio and TV we keep hearing about the atom bomb, the hydrogen bomb, and the analgesic bomb. *Analgesic* — explosive."

pedantic

Can you analyze in similar fashion the little learning and the lines of thought leading to the deductions below? Help is provided in a footnote, but you are protected against a quick look.

misanthrope

misanthrope	the wrong man
innate	never having lived
indigent	innumerable

The more circuitous the route leading to a definition, the more gratifying it is to follow it through. Compare your explanations of the meanings below with those in the footnote. Yours may be even more logical.

impervious	just lately
pensive	cheap
dissimulation	indigestion
antipodes	caterpillars
deciduous	twelfth

antipodes

The strange usage of a word, without definition, presents a double challenge. One must determine *both* the assumption leading to the usage *and* the little learning accounting for the assumption.

"She tried many reducing diets, but remained indefatigable."
in — not, as in *ineffective*; de — off, as in *decapitate*; fat — fat; able — able; *indefatigable — unable to take the fat off.*

"The Club voted her their most homogeneous housewife."
homo — home; genius — smart person; *homogeneous — smart as a home-maker.*

ANSWERS:

WORD	PROBABLE STUDENT REASONING
misanthrope	"mis — wrong (*mistake*); anthrop — man (*anthropology*); *wrong man*"
innate	"in — not (*insecure*); nat — born (*natal*); *not born*"
indigent	"in — not (*inhuman*); dig — number (*digit*); *numberless*"
impervious	"in — not (*impossible*); per — same as *pre*; per — same as previous; impervious — not previous; *just lately*"
pensive	"ex — no longer (*ex-senator*); expensive — no longer pensive; pensive — *cheap*"
dissimulation	"dissent — opposite of assent; dissimulation — opposite of assimilation; assimilation — complete digestion; dissimulation — *indigestion*"
antipodes	"anti — against (*antislavery*); pod — foot (*tripod*) antipodes — creatures with feet against bodies; *caterpillars*"
deciduous	"dec — ten (*decade*); du — two (*duet*) *deciduous — twelfth*"

48   LITTLE LEARNING

"The parents were trying hard to teach their pigeon-toed child to expedite."

ex — out, as in *exit;* ped — feet, as in centipede; *expedite — turn the feet outward; toe out.*

"The chief purpose of their propaganda was insinuation, especially among the youth of the land."

in — into, as in *insert,* sin — sin; *insinuation* — indoctrination with sin, or *promoting crime.*

"We were taught discursive writing in the first grade."

dis — not, as in *discomfort;* cursive writing — joined together; *discursive writing* — not joined together; *printing.*

Obviously, students do think their way through a problem. Could adults confronted with an unfamiliar word make a better showing? Ask a group of adults to define a few words *they* are unlikely to have met — *telemaniac* and *pantophobia,* for example — and compare their interpretations with these student definitions:

telemaniac	one who can't keep a secret; one constantly on the phone; reporter anxious to get a scoop; a terrible gossip; a screaming idiot
pantophobia	fear of shortness of breath; stage fright, especially about pantomimes; wearing suspenders and belt, both

RIGHT-AND-WRONG

An engaging offshoot of the Little Learning group combines right definitions with wrong applications:

WORD	RIGHT STUDENT DEFINITION	WRONG APPLICATION
risqué	daring	"The risqué little squirrel wasn't afraid of the dog."
senility	old age	"Redwoods are noted for their senility."
verbose	full of words	"The dictionary is verbose."
docile	easily taught	"Shakespeare is not very docile."
affable	pleasant	"What an affable morning!"
hoi polloi	the masses	"Our neighbor's whole family went to hoi polloi on Easter Sunday."

WORD	RIGHT DEFINITION	WRONG APPLICATION
imminent	threatening	"The bully was approaching the boy in an imminent manner."
indefatigable	tireless	"The Hallowe'en gang left several cars indefatigable."
apathetic	without feeling	"Simon Legree beat his slaves apathetically."
prolific	multiplying fast	"Jack is the most prolific boy in his grade, but Ralph can add faster."
disparaging	running down	"Our caller talked for two hours with no sign of disparaging."

imminent

Some right-and-wrong combinations go even further:

apropos	opportune	"Aproposity knocks only once."
alias	otherwise	"John will preside if he can attend the meeting. Alias, I'll have to."

An unexpected usage may reveal an incongruous sense of proportion:

"The pyromaniac committed one crime after another because he hoped to go to Hell."

"The miser hid his money because he believed in reincarnation."

"Aeneas showed strength of character, not weakness, when he left Dido, for not many men would give up a kingdom, and the woman they loved, just to accommodate the gods."

"The astronomer decided to move to a high mountain, to be nearer his work."

LINGUISTIC LABYRINTH

Closely related to the Right-and-Wrong Pullet Surprises are those resulting not from misinterpretation but from a struggle to cope with language itself. For example, those who wrote the following definitions knew what they were talking about:

WORD	TEEN-AGER DEFINITION
symphony	nice noise
research	very studiful work
concave	unround
invaluable	the price exceeds more than anything
sardonic	very sneerlike
analogy	small sameness

WORD	TEEN-AGER DEFINITION
hypocrite	saying they are against and then doing it theirself
asterisk	a kind of bristly period
alternate	the other one of something

A reader inclined to be critical of such student efforts might try to define a few entirely familiar words from his morning paper. He, too, might find the language somewhat unwieldy.

A student's idea may somehow get through, though subjected to severe linguistic strain:

"The beauty of the scene marveled everybody."
"She is a chronic ailer."

But a thought may be all but lost:

monetary	assigned to do so
shibboleth	a word in the Bible that caused the death of many lives

Mistaken or uncertain ideas are further obscured, of course, by linguistic limitations:

WORD	TEEN-AGER DEFINITION
deference	the opposite of being the same
perimeter	the amount around the outside of anything
biweekly	happening every two times a week
condolence	grieveness
eccentricity	something extremely like itself

Linguistic difficulty compounded with muddled thinking produced:

incumbent	person trying to hold an office he already holds
paragon	a five-sided triangle
paleolithic	aged, but not old
genuflection	act of bowing from the knees
posterity	ancestors who will come after you
diatribe	a two shaped group
stalemate	agreement that can't be agreed upon
homogeneous	two things that resemble the other
tripod	a three-footed animal

genuflection

At times the linguistic labyrinth has proved too much:

"A hypocrite is some one who thinks he is some one of whom he isn't."

"The girl which was a stowaway got into the United States by a pseudonym which she later had to tell her right name."

"We tried to palliate the man's fears, but only in vain did we dare succeed."

On the other hand, some students are far from inept verbally. Few adults could equal the studied delicacy of

psychic	what one takes at home
cursory	not saying the right thing
enigma	something to correct faulty illumination
delinquent	one who hasn't had good care

In the Guessing Games below, a "little learning" has provided the starting point for each student definition. Following the type of reasoning illustrated in the earlier pages of this chapter, match words and definitions. "Answers," on page 53, are the speculations of the author as to the probable sources of the student conclusions. Readers may suggest a line of reasoning even more plausible.

chiropodist

PULLET SURPRISE GUESSING GAME 30

COLUMN A			COLUMN B
WORD			STUDENT DEFINITION
1. inventory	( )	a.	put out the lights
2. autocracy	( )	b.	medieval history
3. pentathlon	( )	c.	ghost town
4. semantics	( )	d.	sun porch
5. macadam	( )	e.	five mile track event
6. pyrotechnics	( )	f.	animal using feet like hands
7. solon	( )	g.	U.S. Patent Office
8. necropolis	( )	h.	science of making ovenware
9. chiropodist	( )	i.	control of car production
10. elucidate	( )	j.	Cain or Abel

pentathlon

	PROBABLE STUDENT REASONING	STUDENT CONCLUSION
1. (g)	*invent*, -ory — place, as in *armory*, *depository*. Place where inventions are deposited	U.S. Patent Office
2. (i)	*auto* — car; -cracy — rule, as in *democracy*	control over car production
3. (e)	*pent* — five, as in *pentagon*; athl—*athletics* or track events	a five-mile track event
4. (b)	*semi* — half, as in *semi*-annual; antic — *antique*	medieval history
5. (j)	*Mac* — son of, as in *MacDonald*; *Macadam* — son of Adam	Cain or Abel
6. (h)	*pyr* — fire, as in *pyrex*; *technics* — science, as in *technical*	science of making oven-ware
7. (d)	*sol* — sun, as in *solar*; *solon*; *uns* — place sun uns on is	sun parlor or porch
8. (c)	*necro* — dead, as in *necrology*; *polis*—city, as in *Annapolis*	ghost town
9. (f)	*chiro* — hand, as in *chirography*; pod — *foot*, as in *tripod*	an animal using feet like hands
10. (a)	*e* — out, as in *emit*; *luc* — light — *lucent*, as in trans-*lucent*	put out the lights

PULLET SURPRISE GUESSING GAME 31

COLUMN A		COLUMN B
WORD		STUDENT DEFINITION
1. avocation	( )	a. half wits
2. contemporary	( )	b. searching for missing persons
3. epicure	( )	c. figure having equal angles
4. bibulous	( )	d. bring to head again
5. impecunious	( )	e. bird song
6. paragon	( )	f. long-lasting
7. mores	( )	g. a dead issue
8. recapitulate	( )	h. rich
9. misanthropic	( )	i. bookish
10. hypothesis	( )	j. one who tells heroic tales

avocation

epicure

PROBABLE STUDENT REASONING	STUDENT CONCLUSION
1. (e) avi — bird, as in *avi*ary; voc — voice, as in *voc*al	bird song
2. (f) con — opposite, as in pro and *con;* temporary — not expected to last long	long-lasting
3. (j) epic — heroic tale	one who tells heroic tales
4. (i) bibl — book, as in *bibl*iomaniac	bookish
5. (h) im — in, as in *im*migrant; pecun — money, as in *pecuni*ary; in the money, rich	rich
6. (c) par — equal, as in *par;* gon — angle, as in poly*gon*	a figure having equal angles
7. (a) moron — a fool	half-wits
8. (d) re — again, as in *re*view; *capit* — head, as in de*capit*ate	bring to a head again
9. (b) mis — miss; anthrop — man or person, as in *anthrop*ology	searching for
10. (g) hypo — a deadener; thesis — something to be argued about, an issue	a dead issue

ANSWERS TO GUESSING GAME 31

THE

NONCHALANT

"Why worry?"

6   The Haphazard

Section III introduces the Pullet Surprises of students distinct in temperament from those responsible for Sections I and II. Section I presented the interpretations of those unaware of distinctions between words, Section II the deductions of those disquieted by awareness and struggling valiantly to find clues to meaning. In Section III we shall meet the Enviably Nonchalant, who when fully aware that they don't know a word refuse to be disturbed. To them an unknown word may be a momentary nuisance but never a challenge. They look for no clues, ponder no likelihoods. They take a chance, hazard a meaning, and plunge ahead. Intuition, they feel, may work as well as reasoning, and is far less bothersome. Resultant misinterpretations are highly individual—and wholly inexplicable:

orthodox	bottom half
laity	indignation
gregarious	beautiful
trite	one's main work

Are such definitions unabashedly zany, or is there some spark of justification which has escaped detection?

reticent	companion
oblivious	topheavy
chaotic	cheerful
hoi polloi	nonsense
ignominy	having only one husband or wife

With the help of the Nonchalant, new personalities emerge:

pathos	a Greek god
pachyderm	a pharmacist
antipodes	a Greek mathematician

chaotic	a very refined person	
infidel	one not able to do much work	
anomaly	one not inclined to talk	

Whether or not students add illustrations of usage, such definitions prompt reader comment:

WORD	STUDENT DEFINITION AND USAGE	READER COMMENT
gullible	brave in action "The men boasted that they had the most gullible general in the army."	(Can this statement go unchallenged?)
cynic	part of a business	(Inevitably.)
epidermis	the part of the body above the abdomen and below the chest	(*Where??*)

Usages alone inspire similar comment:

STUDENT USAGE	READER COMMENT
"Betty was in a cadaverous and carefree mood."	(A fatalist?)
"The pachyderm was located in the small of the back."	(Eureka!)
"The dramatics class put on a very good apathy."	(Classes can.)
"Our acerbity is just east of the old canyon, about ten miles back."	(An excellent location. Let's leave it there.)

7 A New Look

BOTH WORDS AND DEFINITIONS sometimes appear with an arresting new look which makes each unique. Their individuality suggests inclusion in Section III, although some of them obviously stem from the categories of other sections. Here the lofty indifference of the Nonchalant extends to a freedom in spelling that creates a special genus of Pullet Surprises. The following are typical:

"The old epics were chanted to the accompaniment of a liar."

"The Constitution guarantees certain rights to citizens of every race and greed."

"In writing themes, be sure to very the adjectives."

"At the market she found a nice friar for Sunday dinner."

"An exhibitionist is one who loves the lime life."

"No one knows the origin of Easter Island's craven images."

"It was her wish to be creamated."

"The best thing for cattle is a good pastor."

"This ointment is good for sore mussels."

"The chauffeur was furious over getting a fine for wreckless driving."

"The actress left the stage in undo haste."

"Grandmother gave her air looms to the Hysterical Society."

"Mr. Conwell is considered one of the finest pedagods on the faculty."

"The award was made posthumorously."

"He smelled the odor of baking long before he interred."

"The editor received an anonymous litter from an indignant citizen."

Reader comment is spontaneous:

"The lieutenant was court-martialed for accepting brides from the enemy."

(Regulations are strict in the Armed Forces.)

"Her difficulties were the result of laps of memory."   (O-o-o-h?)

"The ailing king finally went into a comma, and died."   (What an ignominious demise!)

The right-and-wrong Pullet Surprise becomes the more challenging when altered by a New Look. An orthodox definition given orally by a teacher is especially likely to undergo a change leading to a perplexing usage:

"The car was about to dishabille."

WORD	TEACHER DEFINITION	STUDENT INTERPRETATION
dishabille	loose attire	lose a tire

If you can figure out similar explanations for the statements that follow, you qualify as a New Look expert. (A footnote provides help for the impatient.)

1. "We felt safe after the car was emeritus."

2. "I was afraid the snake would wince and strike."

3. "After three months the laundry sells all unjustifiable garments."

4. "The scouts' banal of meeting was the old town hall."

5. "We took our sandwiches, but the lemonade was melee."

6. "The pet goat had to be sold because of constant refutation of the children."

7. "He was the first miner to stake out extol."

8. "The photographer couldn't get Jimmy to stalemate."

9. "Jack Horner sat in the corner and pulled out savoir-faire."

refutation

To cope with the New Look in the Guessing Games that follow, you will need discernment and imagination. Solutions are complicated by the combination of the New Look with Blurrish, Mistaken Identity, and Noble Effort. Furthermore, the New Look may appear in either column or in both columns of a Guessing Game.

ANSWERS:

WORD	TEACHER DEFINITION	STUDENT INTERPRETATION
1. *emeritus*	retired	re-tired
2. *wince*	recoil	re-coil
3. *unjustifiable*	uncalled for	not called for
4. *banal*	commonplace	common place
5. *melee*	free-for-all	free for all
6. *refutation*	rebuttal	re-buttal
7. *extol*	acclaim	a claim
8. *stalemate*	standstill	stand still
9. *savoir-faire*	aplomb	a plum

60   A NEW LOOK

As in previous Guessing Games, after each word in Column A write the letter designating the most likely definition in Column B. For example, after *etymology*, below, your choice should be *d*. Answers at the bottom of each page give only matching numbers and letters. Games 36 to 39 of the New Look type, with answers, will be found in the Appendix.

PULLET SURPRISE GUESSING GAME 32

COLUMN A		COLUMN B
WORD		TEEN-AGER DEFINITION
1. etymology	( )	a. fall air
2. escalator	( )	b. funeral writes
3. succor	( )	c. of course
4. a la carte	( )	d. study of the etym bum
5. obsequies	( )	e. hotter
6. atheist	( )	f. a knitwit
7. surly	( )	g. rolling stares
8. inherent	( )	h. in the days of shiverless knighthood
9. toreador	( )	i. according to the bill affair
10. feudal	( )	j. one who doesn't believe in God, and will more in lightly go to Hell

feudal

PULLET SURPRISE GUESSING GAME 33

COLUMN A		COLUMN B
WORD		TEEN-AGER DEFINITION
1. acrid	( )	a. not allowed to pertisitate
2. orgy	( )	b. high on mighty; snubbish
3. burrough	( )	c. make feel like egurgitatin
4. waive	( )	d. burying a human been
5. robot	( )	e. wish you hadn't
6. arrogant	( )	f. a friendly jester
7. nauseate	( )	g. pittr
8. interment	( )	h. drunken rebelry
9. ineligible	( )	i. canoe or raff
10. surrey	( )	j. little dunky

waive

burrough

ANSWERS TO GUESSING GAMES:

GAME 32	GAME 33
1. d	1. g
2. g	2. h
3. f	3. j
4. i	4. f
5. b	5. i
6. j	6. b
7. c	7. c
8. a	8. d
9. e	9. a
10. h	10. e

Pullet Surprise Guessing Game 34

Column A			Column B
WORD			TEEN-AGER DEFINITION
1. termite	(	)	a. jubilant delinquent
2. solar	(	)	b. a fast drip
3. reincarnation	(	)	c. far retching
4. Charon	(	)	d. rays from son
5. extensive	(	)	e. sweetheart
6. commune	(	)	f. servant in Dark Ages
7. treacle	(	)	g. guy who helped folks across the sticks
8. adolescent	(	)	h. aunt that eats wood
9. naive	(	)	i. go back and forth to the subburgs
10. louvre	(	)	j. return in new bean

solar

Pullet Surprise Guessing Game 35

Column A			Column B
WORD			TEEN-AGER DEFINITION
1. tourney	(	)	a. opposite of brethren
2. stigma	(	)	b. not hittin fare
3. urchin	(	)	c. from fawn country
4. slogan	(	)	d. mild tempter
5. prognosticate	(	)	e. wherly
6. strident	(	)	f. prswadin
7. align	(	)	g. something tinkling in the Bible
8. cistern	(	)	h. prog up nose
9. symbol	(	)	i. word in frat names, like Stigma New and Cap a Stigma
10. tepid	(	)	j. earitating

symbol

Answers to Guessing Games:

GAME 34		GAME 35	
1.	h	1.	e
2.	d	2.	i
3.	j	3.	f
4.	g	4.	b
5.	c	5.	h
6.	i	6.	j
7.	b	7.	c
8.	a	8.	a
9.	f	9.	g
10.	e	10.	d

THE

TRUSTING

"You just take it for granite!"

8 Take-It-For-Granites

"YOU DON'T HAVE TO LOOK up new words," asserts a lad. "You can just take for granite what they mean from the way they're used."

Assuming meanings from context is a dangerous practice, beginning in childhood and often continuing throughout adulthood. Students who put their trust in usage frequently quote a familiar phrase in support of a definition:

paragon	upholder, as in "a paragon of virtue"
analgesic	rubbing, as in "analgesic ointment"

Faith in context engenders a strong sense of security. The word *incumbent* came up in a high school class. Members were in complete accord as to its meaning: it meant a scoundrel. In spirited defense of their conviction they cited a current city campaign. A local newspaper was strongly opposing re-election of the mayor, and was promoting the candidacy of a new man.

"*Incumbent* MUST mean a scoundrel," insisted a student. "Last night's Tribune said that Mr. Davis has done all kinds of good things for the community, while Mr. Lee, THE INCUMBENT, has never done a thing. (As uttered, there was no mistaking the meaning of *incumbent*. It *had* to mean scoundrel.)

Such classroom incidents are legion. A key word in a statement yields a surprising range of plausible "for-granite" interpretations:

"The doctor had a long talk with the parents about their son's chronic ailment."

chronic	serious; contagious; imaginary; incurable; heart; lung; stomach

"The reporters call Taylor the most versatile man on the team."

versatile	speedy; clever; dependable; popular

Unfortunately, subsequent contexts are likely to add validity to an erroneous deduction. All meanings of *chronic* given above could reasonably be applied to *chronic pain*, a *chronic condition*, a *chronic difficulty*; those of *versatile* to a *versatile salesman,* or a *versatile writer.* If *gregarious,* in the phrase *gregarious people,* is taken to mean vicious, curious, active, happy, or colorful, a later reference to *gregarious animals* or to *gregarious instincts* will strengthen the original interpretation.

Familiar usages are no guarantee against mistaken notions. To a "for-graniter," *extenuating* circumstances may be embarrassing, enlightening, or incriminating; a *garrulous* old fellow may be shabby, greedy, or mean; an *eon* ago may mean a hundred years, ten years, two weeks, or a thousand years; a person treated like a *pariah* may be made to feel like a prince, a priest, or a god.

A derogatory context is especially prolific. An unbelievable number of uncomplimentary meanings are likely to be ascribed to a single word. Moreover, a misinterpretation of a term of reproach has exceptional tenacity. It will weather context after context:

hypocrite	smart-aleck; snob; braggart; fool; liar; loafer; fanatic; sneak; beatnik; tightwad; Communist; ignoramus; sponger

A "for-graniter" seldom checks an assumption. It isn't laziness that deters; it's self-respect. To seek verification of an assumption would be to him a confession of inadequacy. Ignoring the dictionary is evidence of selfsufficiency, resourcefulness. The products of do-it-yourself efficiency are to a "for-graniter" wholly acceptable.

Only occasionally does an interpretation long taken for granted come suddenly into question. For example, thanks largely to Hollywood, student assurance in defining *exotic* is almost universal:

exotic	breathtakingly beautiful; glamorous; dreamy; alluring

Certainty of such meaning continues until by chance a broadcast reports that a number of exotic reptiles have been acquired by a zoo, or a traveler describes as exotic the custom of wearing nose rings. In such case a "for-graniter" may be shocked even into consulting a dictionary.

Any misapprehension is likely to start a chain of errors. A context leads to an assumption, which leads to an application, which leads to a further assumption, and so on and on:

CONTEXT:	The historian accorded equal praise to the contemporary generals, Grant and Lee.
ASSUMPTION:	*contemporary*—fighting each other
APPLICATION:	"It's unfortunate when two or more nations are contemporary."
CONTEXT:	His father gave a feast for the prodigal.
ASSUMPTION:	*prodigal*—favorite son
APPLICATION:	"The various states nominated their prodigals for the vice-presidency."

CONTEXT:	That shop was the choice of hoi polloi
ASSUMPTION:	*hoi polloi*—high society
APPLICATION:	"Who does she think she is—one of the hoi polloi?"

The potential impairment to understanding and to communication for which context is responsible is inestimable. In the areas of social and moral values "for-granite" assumptions may well arouse concern:

CONTEXT:	The young man was recommended for the position because of his integrity.
INTERPRETATIONS:	*integrity* ambition; pull, smartness; originality; common sense; ability; ability to get ahead of the other fellow; playing politics
CONTEXT:	The topic under discussion was the juvenile delinquent.
INTERPRETATIONS:	*delinquent* any one under twenty-one years of age; one who hasn't been turned in; an untrained person; innocent, yet damaging
CONTEXT:	We agreed that the proposed procedure would be ethical.
INTERPRETATIONS:	*ethical* logical; legal; sensible; advantageous; practical; clever; excusable; etiquette

One of the meanings above will account for each of these otherwise surprising statements:

"It isn't ethical to eat with your knife."

"They accused him of integrity."

"There are seven delinquents in our family. I'm the fifth one."

For-granite assumptions may be arresting:

precocious	dangerous
condolence	congratulation
conjugal	disagreeing
construe	turn to one's own advantage
philanthropist	one who gives back all he has taken
incumbent	one carried along with no effort on his part

They may be alarming, even dangerous:

toxic	good for one; exhilarating; medicinal
inflammable	not burning easily

Or they may be unexpectedly apt:

delude	make happy
plutocrat	a single man
compunction	afterthought
misogynist	one who saves money
monogamous	monotonous
ethical	possible, but not probable
stalemate	government program
unique	on time
posterity	life after death
senility	reality
epitaph	finishing lines
polygamy	versatility

The following Guessing Game differs in character from those of previous chapters. Try here to match words with definitions *and* to supply a plausible context to substantiate each choice. Obviously, no answers can be provided for such a game. One guess may be as good as another.

PULLET SURPRISE GUESSING GAME 40

COLUMN A		COLUMN B
WORD		DEFINITION
1. amphibious ( )		a. incompetent
2. trite ( )		b. X-ray
3. nauseate ( )		c. a writer
4. eulogy ( )		d. big storm
5. incumbent ( )		e. to the point
6. anon ( )		f. original
7. holocaust ( )		g. political speech
8. enervating ( )		h. annoy unbearably
9. eccentric ( )		i. bracing
10. nebulous ( )		j. elderly

9 Chameleon Words

THE PERILS OF CONTEXT are abundantly evident in the preceding chapter. Clearly, any unknown word is a chameleon, taking a deceptive coloring from its immediate environment. But color that is temporary ought not to be associated inseparably with any one chameleon, and the meaning lent by environment should not be identified with any one word.

So strong is our tendency to depend on context, however, that we must be consciously on guard against its influence. As Nature abhors a vacuum, so the mind cannot abide a word without meaning. Imagination rushes to fill the void by drawing from its surroundings. When, rarely, an unfamiliar word is met with no context, the mind instantly improvises a setting to invest it with meaning. As an illuminating experiment, try a group or family game which can be played at any vocabulary level. "Humpty Dumpty said to Alice, 'When I use a word it means just what I choose it to mean—neither more nor less'." The game may well be called *Humpty Dumpty*.

To play *Humpty Dumpty*, browse through a dictionary. Find a word new to you and unlikely to be known to the others of the group—preferably a word of not more than three syllables. Announce and spell the word, without defining it. Ask each player to write a sentence using the word *as he interprets it*. In one adult group the word *calkin* was typically productive:

> "It was June, and the calkins were singing in the maples."
> "Mounting his spirited calkin, he cantered away."
> "In Ireland, all the children know that it's the calkins and the leprechauns that get them into mischief."
> "Ours was as proud a crew as ever sailed a calkin."
> "The daisies were already in bloom, but the tiny calkins were just peeping through the ground."
> " 'Lullaby, my little calkin,' sang the mother to her child."
> "To summon the clan, he blew three long blasts on his calkin."
> "The wrinkled old calkin put a curse on the family."

"The white bark of the tall calkins was a contrast to the dark pines."

"For dessert, try freshly baked calkins with cheese."

"Anyone could tell a McTavish, from the jaunty way be wore his calkin."

"Finally, the old woman lost patience entirely. 'You little calkin!' she screamed."

Such a demonstration of the chameleon nature of words is provocative. One is tempted to try *using* single words as variously interpreted by students. A few of the following definitions have appeared in earlier chapters, as results of mistaken identity, noble effort, or context:

WORD	STUDENT DEFINITION	READER APPLICATION
peccadillo	a bird	A pair of peccadillos had nested in the cherry tree.
	a stringed instrument	He was learning to play the peccadillo.
	a London street	I saw it in a little Peccadillo shop.
hoi polloi	infantile paralysis	Everyone should be immunized against hoi polloi.
	nonsense	Such arguments are sheer hoi polloi.
	a Chinese name	The laundry is run by Hoi Polloi.
	a college fraternity	Seven freshmen were initiated into Hoi Polloi.
	a Hawaiian food	Did the islanders serve you hoi polloi at the luau?
	hello	Friendly persons greet one another with "*HOI*, polloi!"

The chameleon character of words can seriously retard the transmission of thought. Paradoxically, however, it makes possible a type of pseudo-communication widely practised. Chameleonese is the more convincing when cumulative in effect.

Woven into the following story are Pullet Surprises of every type mentioned in this book. The individual Surprises are listed, in order of occurrence, on page 72. You will find the story more effective, however, if *before* consulting the list you plunge into the reading, trusting to context and suspense to carry you through. Read this moving tale *aloud,* rapidly, dramatically, and it will carry conviction. It is offered as a final, composite, omnibus PULLET SURPRISE.

THE CHIVERLESS KNIGHT

David, who had grown up in a pedantry, was always reading about the days of Chiverless Knighthood, and dreaming up stories in which he himself played a heroic role. In one he was strolling through a woodland, strumming his peccadillo, when he came to a shady arbitrary in which a beautiful maiden was gathering colorful chameleons and weaving them into garlands.

Suddenly, a huge orthodox charged out of the woods straight toward the maiden. There was no time for the knight to be precocious. What needed to be done would have to be done spuriously. With drawn poignant he advanced stridently toward the orthodox, which at sight of him stopped short, nostrils dilatory, and seemed to expiate fire from its mouth. But the only thought of the shiverless knight was to emaciate the maiden from the orthodox. Carefully he matriculated around the lugubrious creature, hoping to get near enough to slash the beast's epigram. Failing this, he ramified a fatal blow at the creature's panacea, and with a holocaust the orthodox fell.

The maiden, who at sight of the terrible incarceration had been monetarily overcome with nostalgia, recovered quickly, and wished to show her gratuity to the knight. At her bequest he accompanied her to the paragon where she lived. Her father, the pariah of the realm, gave a huge fiasco in honor of the hero. Her fiancé, indigent over the favor accorded the knight, plotted to have the newcomer expedited, and even planned a niggardly murder. But the plot was flustrated, and in his disparity the thwarted suitor plunged a dagger into his epitome and shortly afterward exhumed.

The pariah, already in his adage, had long been looking for a man of sufficient inertia and ambiguity to take his place, and with the anonymous consent of his whole diatribe he gave his realm and his daughter to the Chiverless Knight.

Pullet Surprises of "The Chiverless Knight"

(in order of their occurrence)

WORD	TEEN-AGER DEFINITION	WORD	TEEN-AGER DEFINITION
chivalrous	chiverless (shiverless)	panacea	organ in pit of stomach
pedantry	children's home	holocaust	roar
peccadillo	stringed instrument	incarceration	slaughter
arbitrary	garden, with trees	monetarily	for the moment
chameleon	a flower	nostalgia	sickness at the stomach
orthodox	a big animal		
precocious	cautious beforehand	gratuity	appreciation
spurious	on the spur of the moment	bequest	asking
		paragon	huge building
alienist	helper; ally	pariah	ruler
onerously	by oneself	fiasco	feast; festival
poignant	dagger; sword	indigent	outraged
strident	walking with purpose	expedite	get rid of
		niggardly	cowardly
dilatory	expanding and contracting	flustrate	block; thwart
		epitome	solar plexus
expiate	spit forth	exhume	breathe one's last
emaciate	set free	adage	advanced age
matriculate	work one's way	inertia	energy
lugubrious	horrible	ambiguity	initiative
epigram	throat	anonymous	all agreed
ramify	attack with force	diatribe	two tribes combined

Appendix

If you're playing a Guessing Game alone, score 10 points for each correct answer. If in competition, give each participant a list of Column B lettered definitions. Read aloud, one at a time, the words of Column A. Participants mark on their lists the matching number, and write after each the word they think the student had in mind. Check your answers with those in the book.

Guessing Games 4 and 5 are of the Mistaken Identity type.

PULLET SURPRISE GUESSING GAME — 4

bizarre

COLUMN A		COLUMN B	
WORD		STUDENT DEFINITION	
1. archaic ( )		a. make last forever ( )
2. orgy ( )		b. rock column in cave ( )
3. paragon ( )		c. powder, rouge, lipstick, etc. ( )
4. bizarre ( )		d. treat metal ( )
5. perpetrate ( )		e. geometric figure ( )
6. stalemate ( )		f. bird of prey ( )
7. temporize ( )		g. far North ( )
8. dauphin ( )		h. a monster ( )
9. eclectic ( )		i. a playful fish ( )
10. cosmic ( )		j. a fit ( )

ANSWERS TO GUESSING GAMES:

GAME 4

1. g (Arctic)
2. h (ogre)
3. e (polygon)
4. f (buzzard)
5. a (perpetuate)
6. b (stalagmite)
7. d (temper)
8. i (dolphin)
9. j (epileptic)
10. c (cosmetic)

dauphin

PULLET SURPRISE GUESSING GAME — 5

COLUMN A			COLUMN B		
WORD			STUDENT DEFINITION		
1. salvage	(	)	a. appetizing	(	)
2. deflect	(	)	b. pain killer	(	)
3. tenure	(	)	c. Jewish	(	)
4. palpable	(	)	d. seasickness	(	)
5. epithet	(	)	e. male singer	(	)
6. nostalgia	(	)	f. midday rest	(	)
7. semantic	(	)	g. imperfection	(	)
8. panegyric	(	)	h. edge of cloth	(	)
9. odious	(	)	i. something on a tombstone	(	)
10. fiasco	(	)	j. strong-smelling	(	)

ANSWERS TO GUESSING GAMES:

GAME 5

1. h (selvage) 6. d (nausea)
2. g (defect) 7. c (Semitic)
3. e (tenor) 8. b (paregoric)
4. a (palatable) 9. j (odorous)
5. i (epitaph) 10. f (siesta)

tenure

fiasco

Games 9 to 13 are of the Blurrish type.

PULLET SURPRISE GUESSING GAME — 9

COLUMN A			COLUMN B		
WORD			STUDENT DEFINITION		
1. arrogate	(	)	a. scrambled eggs	(	)
2. ricochet	(	)	b. what one is sent on	(	)
3. gremlin	(	)	c. not trusting	(	)
4. amulet	(	)	d. one after another	(	)
5. coronation	(	)	e. a swing you lie down on	(	)
6. auspicious	(	)	f. turn water onto land	(	)
7. scourge	(	)	g. a spicy flower	(	)
8. secession	(	)	h. a Chinese cart	(	)
9. errant	(	)	i. almost burn	(	)
10. hummock	(	)	j. center of Soviet government	(	)

ANSWERS TO GUESSING GAMES:

GAME 9

1. f (irrigate) 6. c (suspicious)
2. h (ricksha) 7. i (scorch)
3. j (Kremlin) 8. d (succession)
4. a (omelet) 9. b (errand)
5. g (carnation) 10. e (hammock)

ricochet

hummock

tyro

PULLET SURPRISE GUESSING GAME — 10

COLUMN A			COLUMN B		
WORD			STUDENT DEFINITION		
1. indigent	(	)	a. a group of three singers	(	)
2. platitude	(	)	b. sweet smelling	(	)
3. overt	(	)	c. disheartening	(	)
4. tyro	(	)	d. driver of some V.I.P.'s car	(	)
5. disparaging	(	)	e. hot and dry	(	)
6. eccentricity	(	)	f. angry; stirred up	(	)
7. desultory	(	)	g. stress on syllable	(	)
8. bibulous	(	)	h. width on a globe	(	)
9. vagrant	(	)	i. a long, narrow circle	(	)
10. chauvinist	(	)	j. having digestive difficulty	(	)

PULLET SURPRISE GUESSING GAME — 11

COLUMN A			COLUMN B		
WORD			STUDENT DEFINITION		
1. brochure	(	)	a. hint; suggest	(	)
2. malleable	(	)	b. turn or coil	(	)
3. anathema	(	)	c. not careful	(	)
4. nadir	(	)	d. use medication in throat	(	)
5. incinerate	(	)	e. Greek goddess of wisdom	(	)
6. gargoyle	(	)	f. no demand for	(	)
7. foible	(	)	g. O.K. with the P.O.	(	)
8. callous	(	)	h. an article of women's apparel	(	)
9. tryst	(	)	i. story about animals	(	)
10. unassailable	(	)	j. not one or the other	(	)

Anathema

ANSWERS TO GUESSING GAMES:

GAME 10

1. f (indignant)
2. h (latitude)
3. i (oval)
4. a (trio)
5. c (discouraging)
6. g (accent)
7. e (sultry)
8. j (bilious)
9. b (fragrant)
10. d (chauffeur)

GAME 11

1. h (brassiere)
2. g (mailable)
3. e (Athena)
4. j (neither)
5. a (insinuate)
6. d (gargle)
7. i (fable)
8. c (careless)
9. b (twist)
10. f (unsalable)

PULLET SURPRISE GUESSING GAME — 12

foray

COLUMN A			COLUMN B		
WORD			STUDENT DEFINITION		
1. ingenuous	(	)	a. permit for divorce	(	)
2. brawn	(	)	b. like a play	(	)
3. chimera	(	)	c. how far	(	)
4. degree	(	)	d. killing germs	(	)
5. synonym	(	)	e. oversized shrimp	(	)
6. irrelevant	(	)	f. to do with redskins	(	)
7. extant	(	)	g. having no respect for religion	(	)
8. foray	(	)	h. what shows doctor what you got	(	)
9. traumatic	(	)	i. kodak	(	)
10. disaffection	(	)	j. a fight	(	)

ingenuous

PULLET SURPRISE GUESSING GAME — 13

bumpkin

COLUMN A			COLUMN B		
WORD			STUDENT DEFINITION		
1. bumpkin	(	)	a. hindrance; nuisance	(	)
2. dissemble	(	)	b. opposite of subtraction	(	)
3. bigot	(	)	c. Jack o' Lantern	(	)
4. dissipate	(	)	d. person 100 years old	(	)
5. incumbent	(	)	e. all in one key	(	)
6. stentorian	(	)	f. question	(	)
7. integrate	(	)	g. faucet	(	)
8. derelict	(	)	h. take apart	(	)
9. monetary	(	)	i. look forward to	(	)
10. edification	(	)	j. large, crane-like machine for lifting	(	)

ANSWERS TO GUESSING GAMES

GAME 12	GAME 13
1. f (Indian)	1. c (pumpkin)
2. e (prawn)	2. h (disassemble)
3. i (camera)	3. g (faucet)
4. a (decree)	4. i (anticipate)
5. h (symptom)	5. a (encumbrance)
6. g (irreverent)	6. d (centenarian)
7. c (extent)	7. f (interrogate)
8. j (fray)	8. j (derrick)
9. b (dramatic)	9. e (monotone)
10. d (disinfection)	10. b (addition)

derelict

Guessing Games 16 to 21 are of the Power of Suggestion type.

PULLET SURPRISE GUESSING GAME — 16

COLUMN A			COLUMN B		
WORD			STUDENT DEFINITION		
1. duplicity	(	)	a. study of historical events	(	)
2. savory	(	)	b. nerve center in stomach	(	)
3. mendacious	(	)	c. stuffiness in nose	(	)
4. analogy	(	)	d. pertaining to missiles	(	)
5. cryptic	(	)	e. like a knight	(	)
6. enervate	(	)	f. able to be fixed	(	)
7. nostalgia	(	)	g. bridge	(	)
8. errant	(	)	h. get on nerves	(	)
9. bombastic	(	)	i. thrifty	(	)
10. epitome	(	)	j. dead and buried	(	)

errant

duplicity

PULLET SURPRISE GUESSING GAME — 17

COLUMN A			COLUMN B		
WORD			STUDENT DEFINITION		
1. plagiarize	(	)	a. high principles of conduct	(	)
2. sonorous	(	)	b. taking every other one	(	)
3. exhortation	(	)	c. treat with ointment	(	)
4. friable	(	)	d. daily feature in newspaper	(	)
5. capitulate	(	)	e. great joy over success	(	)
6. altruism	(	)	f. sleeping out loud	(	)
7. ideology	(	)	g. throw with a machine	(	)
8. vacillate	(	)	h. annoy	(	)
9. galaxy	(	)	i. able to be cooked quickly	(	)
10. calumny	(	)	j. extremely polite to women	(	)

galaxy

exhortation

ANSWERS TO GUESSING GAMES:

GAME 16	GAME 17
1. g (duplicate)	1. h (plague)
2. i (save)	2. f (snore)
3. f (mend)	3. e (exult)
4. a (annals)	4. i (fry)
5. j (crypt)	5. g (catapult)
6. h (nerve)	6. b (alternate)
7. c (nostril)	7. a (ideals)
8. e (knight errant)	8. c (vaseline)
9. d (bomb)	9. j (gallantry)
10. b (pit)	10. d (columnist)

COLUMN A			COLUMN B		
WORD			STUDENT DEFINITION		
1. querulous	(	)	a. study of skin disorders	(	)
2. sagacious	(	)	b. shattered	(	)
3. cadaverous	(	)	c. picking a fight	(	)
4. ignominy	(	)	d. having no flavor	(	)
5. noisome	(	)	e. pretty much of a heel	(	)
6. fractious	(	)	f. forbidden	(	)
7. intangible	(	)	g. loud	(	)
8. ichthyology	(	)	h. dwarfishness	(	)
9. chicanery	(	)	i. being scaredy-cat	(	)
10. banal	(	)	j. describing cowboy country	(	)

querulous

ignominy

COLUMN A			COLUMN B		
WORD			STUDENT DEFINITION		
1. empirical	(	)	a. in a hurry	(	)
2. restive	(	)	b. not having to go to war yet	(	)
3. criterion	(	)	c. belonging to the human race	(	)
4. augury	(	)	d. touchiness; temper	(	)
5. evanescent	(	)	e. wanting world power	(	)
6. risibility	(	)	f. officer in Caesar's army	(	)
7. scurrilous	(	)	g. leveling up	(	)
8. homogeneous	(	)	h. boring holes in wood	(	)
9. ideology	(	)	i. comfortable; upholstered	(	)
10. deference	(	)	j. hero worship	(	)

restive

ANSWERS TO GUESSING GAMES:

GAME 19

1. e (empire)
2. i (rest)
3. f (centurion)
4. h (anger)
5. g (even)
6. d (rise)
7. a (scurry)
8. c (genus homo)
9. j (idol)
10. b (deferment)

GAME 18

1. c (quarrel)
2. j (sage)
3. e (cad)
4. h (gnome)
5. g (noise)
6. b (fraction)
7. d (tang)
8. a (itch)
9. i (chicken)
10. f (ban)

augury

Pullet Surprise Guessing Game — 20

	Column A			Column B		
	WORD			STUDENT DEFINITION		
1.	penurious	( )	a.	tardy	( )
2.	doggerel	( )	b.	full of holes	( )
3.	fatuous	( )	c.	imprisoned	( )
4.	enigma	( )	d.	snarling	( )
5.	punctilious	( )	e.	describing a cock fight	( )
6.	duplicity	( )	f.	tied up	( )
7.	latent	( )	g.	destined	( )
8.	overt	( )	h.	making copies; Xeroxing	( )
9.	stringent	( )	i.	mark of disgrace	( )
10.	spurious	( )	j.	Roger	( )

spurious

Pullet Surprise Guessing Game — 21

	Column A			Column B		
	WORD			STUDENT DEFINITION		
1.	suppliant	( )	a.	waving in the breeze	( )
2.	chaparal	( )	b.	something that lives off of something else	( )
3.	levity	( )	c.	having hay fever	( )
4.	entomology	( )	d.	cowboy	( )
5.	nauseated	( )	e.	oil producing	( )
6.	profiteer	( )	f.	a substitute	( )
7.	flagrant	( )	g.	general public	( )
8.	paradox	( )	h.	noncommissioned officer	( )
9.	corpulent	( )	i.	study of burial practices	( )
10.	pompous	( )	j.	one who predicts	( )

flagrant

Answers to Guessing Games:

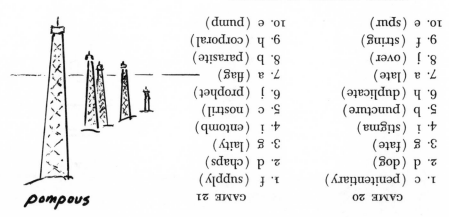

GAME 20	GAME 21
1. c (penitentiary)	1. f (supply)
2. d (dog)	2. d (chaps)
3. g (fate)	3. g (laity)
4. i (stigma)	4. i (entomb)
5. b (puncture)	5. c (nostril)
6. h (duplicate)	6. j (prophet)
7. a (late)	7. a (flag)
8. j (over)	8. b (parasite)
9. f (string)	9. h (corporal)
10. e (spur.)	10. e (pump)

pompous

Guessing Games 26 to 29 are of the Noble Effort type.

PULLET SURPRISE GUESSING GAME 26

COLUMN A		COLUMN B
WORD		STUDENT DEFINITION

marital

1. ambrosia ( ) a. violating parole
2. peerless ( ) b. study of North Pole area
3. illegible ( ) c. party given to pay social obligations
4. marital ( ) d. feminine of Ambrose
5. implacable ( ) e. no commercials
6. carte blanche ( ) f. to do with horses (female)
7. repartee ( ) g. unemployable
8. inadvertent ( ) h. poorly egible
9. topography ( ) i. car with no accessories whatever
10. recrimination ( ) j. can't see

PULLET SURPRISE GUESSING GAME 27

COLUMN A		COLUMN B
WORD		STUDENT DEFINITION

1. gazette ( ) a. keeping weight down
2. squalor ( ) b. not having to be sent to an institution
3. syntax ( ) c. short for press agent
4. canonical ( ) d. wide-eyed girl
5. presage ( ) e. backward
6. stalemate ( ) f. toy cart
7. untoward ( ) g. using heavy artillery
8. cartel ( ) h. heavy fine for wrong-doer
9. noncommittal ( ) i. partner past his prime
10. ungainly ( ) j. cry-baby

cartel

ANSWERS TO GUESSING GAMES:

ungainly

GAME 27	GAME 26
1. d	1. d
2. j	2. j
3. h	3. h
4. g	4. f
5. c	5. g
6. i	6. i
7. e	7. c
8. f	8. e
9. b	9. b
10. a	10. a

Pullet Surprise Guessing Game 28

	Column A		Column B
	WORD		STUDENT DEFINITION
1.	burnish	( )	a. a single tary
2.	dilatory	( )	b. uncover trickery
3.	nonplus	( )	c. remedy for epi
4.	sibilant	( )	d. a female camel
5.	camellia	( )	e. easily ignited
6.	monetary	( )	f. ballooning
7.	epicure	( )	g. nearing a deadline
8.	overt	( )	h. able to fortell
9.	lackadaisical	( )	i. upside down
10.	extricate	( )	j. minus

camellia

overt

Pullet Surprise Guessing Game 29

	Column A		Column B
	WORD		STUDENT DEFINITION
1.	peerage	( )	a. a baby ram
2.	bibliophile	( )	b. having no hills
3.	orgy	( )	c. ad-libbing
4.	conjuror	( )	d. conference room for critics
5.	ramekin	( )	e. age of fusel oil
6.	levity	( )	f. old enough for bifocals
7.	expostulate	( )	g. a con man on a jury
8.	criterion	( )	h. short for organization
9.	fuselage	( )	i. pass ex post facto law
10.	libation	( )	j. Bible section of a library

bibliophile

Answers to Guessing Games:

	GAME 28		GAME 29
1.	e	1.	f
2.	f	2.	j
3.	j	3.	h
4.	h	4.	g
5.	d	5.	a
6.	a	6.	b
7.	c	7.	i
8.	i	8.	d
9.	g	9.	e
10.	b	10.	c

Games 36 to 39 are of the New Look type.

PULLET SURPRISE GUESSING GAME 36

COLUMN A		COLUMN B
WORD		TEEN-AGER DEFINITION
1. anemic	( )	a. long necked animal
2. oboe	( )	b. morless crazy
3. bolero	( )	c. twice weakly
4. eulogy	( )	d. beggar; tramp
5. pogrom	( )	e. expert boler
6. extradite	( )	f. pail
7. psychic	( )	g. little halloween nimp
8. globulin	( )	h. one of our four fathers
9. semiweekly	( )	i. praise of some one, usually diseased
10. graph	( )	j. dite for gaining wait

bolero

PULLET SURPRISE GUESSING GAME 37

COLUMN A		COLUMN B
WORD		TEEN-AGER DEFINITION
1. tenant	( )	a. tarrify
2. reflex	( )	b. football teem
3. obituary	( )	c. cludder
4. leaven	( )	d. border or rumor
5 eccentric	( )	e. moth before metamortified
6. skier	( )	f. fun with rod and lyen
7. calorie	( )	g. old foggy
8. pupa	( )	h. what a mere does
9. fission	( )	i. cheapest seats in the theayter
10. litter	( )	j. summerizing life

graph

leaven

ANSWERS TO GUESSING GAMES:

fission

GAME 36	GAME 37
1. f	1. d
2. d	2. h
3. e	3. j
4. i	4. b
5. h	5. g
6. j	6. a
7. b	7. i
8. g	8. e
9. c	9. f
10. a	10. c

PULLET SURPRISE GUESSING GAME 38

COLUMN A			COLUMN B
WORD			**TEEN-AGER DEFINITION**
1. abominable	(	)	a. bonny
2. improvise	(	)	b. skin with fir
3. rabid	(	)	c. behind the seens
4. smug	(	)	d. belonging to Peru
5. catacombs	(	)	e. cuperate
6. chauvinism	(	)	f. use makeship
7. pellet	(	)	g. smarty fogg
8. convalesce	(	)	h. pushin and chauvin
9. peruse	(	)	i. able to be bommed
10. covert	(	)	j. berrying place for kings like pharomids

peruse

PULLET SUPRISE GUESSING GAME 39

COLUMN A			COLUMN B
WORD			**TEEN-AGER DEFINITION**
1. bauble	(	)	a. Ben Joe
2. saline	(	)	b. upsurd
3. psychiatry	(	)	c. reck
4. forum	(	)	d. make symotaneous
5. ludicrous	(	)	e. hollo soap
6. divan	(	)	f. figger
7. catarrh	(	)	g. mental ferapy
8. synchronize	(	)	h. jump from high place
9. coalition	(	)	i. shopper who doesn't buy
10. lucre	(	)	j. ridin in a boat

divan

ANSWERS TO GUESSING GAMES:

GAME 38	GAME 39
1. i	1. e
2. f	2. j
3. a	3. g
4. g	4. f
5. j	5. b
6. h	6. h
7. b	7. a
8. e	8. d
9. d	9. c
10. c	10. i

Colophon

This book is typeset in 10 point Caledonia
Headline type is Palatino, roman and italic
Paper is Garamond Text, 60-pound
Design by Dana Cordrey, Sultana Press
Cover art by James Graves, Fullerton
Composition and lithography by
  Sultana Press / Premier Printing Company
Binding by Pacific Library Binding Company, Los Angeles